Electric Cooker (

The Best Collection of Electric Pressure Cooker Recipes from Around the World

Legal & Disclaimer

Table of Contents

Recipe 1 – Classical Minestrone Soup

Minestrone is a traditional soup from norther Italy; it is very healthy and it contains very few calories. Traditionally, it is eaten on a Friday night, but of course you can have it whenever you want, even chilled.

Ingredients

- 300 grams (10 oz) of cannellini beans
- A medium sized courgette
- A large onion
- A stalk of celery
- 300 grams (10 oz) of potatoes
- A large carrot
- 3 cloves of garlic
- A tablespoon (20 ml) of extra virgin olive oil
- 600 ml (20 oz) of chicken stock

- 300 ml (10 oz) of vegetable stock
- A small sprig of parsley
- Salt and pepper

Serves 4

Preparation

Wash and slice the courgette (into 1 cm slices).

Peel and chop the onion roughly.

Peel and slice the garlic cloves.

Rinse the cannellini beans.

Peel and cut the potatoes into small cubes (2 cm or 1 inch in size).

Wash and chop the celery stalk.

Peel and cut the carrot into slices (1 cm or ½ inch thick).

Put the onion, the garlic, the celery and the carrot into your pressure cooker.

Add the extra virgin olive oil and sauté for about 10 minutes.

Add the cannellini beans, the potatoes and the courgettes.

Add the chicken stock and the vegetable stock.

Season and seal the pressure cooker.

Cook for approximately 25 minutes.

Chop the parsley and garnish the minestrone before serving.

Recipe 2 – Egg Steamed Rice

Here is a very typical, and what matters more, light, side dish from the orient that you can prepare with your pressure cooker.

Ingredients

- 300 grams (10 oz) of long grain rice
- 2 medium sized eggs
- 150 grams (5 oz) of ham, in a single slice
- 120 grams (4 oz) of bean sprouts
- 150 grams (5 oz) of garden peas
- 450 ml (15 oz) of water
- 1 tablespoon (20 ml) of sunflower oil
- A dash of dark soy sauce

Serves 4

Preparation

Cut the ham into very small squares.

Put the sunflower oil into the pressure cooker.

Heat on medium fire until the oil is sizzling.

Crack the eggs and add them to the sunflower oil.

Scramble the egg for about 3 minutes, mixing continuously.

Add the rice.

Add the water.

Seal the pressure cooker and cook for 12 minutes.

Remove the lid, add the ham and the peas and cook for another 5 minutes, or until the water has fully evaporated.

Serve with a dash of soy sauce (on the side, if you wish).

Recipe 3 – Chard Soup with Barley

If you can find chard, which is only available in large supermarkets and in farmers' markets, it has a very sweet taste, but it is absolutely healthy.

Ingredients

- 400 grams (13 oz) of fresh chard
- 200 grams (7 oz) of dry barley
- 150 grams (5 oz) of potatoes
- 5 cloves of garlic
- 1 large onion
- 600 ml (a pint) of vegetable soup
- A tablespoon of extra virgin olive oil
- Salt and pepper

Serves 4

Preparation

Soak the barley in lukewarm water for about 1 hour.

Peel the potatoes and cut them into small cubes (1 inch or about 2 cm in size).

Peel and chop the onion finely.

Peel and crush the garlic.

Wash and cut the chop the chard roughly.

Put the extra virgin olive oil into the pressure cooker and heat on medium fire.

Add the onion and the garlic, season and sauté the onion and garlic for about 10 minutes.

In the meantime, drain the barley.

Add the chard, the chopped potatoes and the barley.

Add the stock, stir and seal the pressure cooker.

Cook for 20 minutes before serving.

Recipe 4 – Riso e bisi

We go back to northern Italy to the most romantic city in the world, Venice, for this recipe; this is actually an adapted version for your pressure cooker, healthy and much easier to prepare than the original, but still as delicious.

Ingredients

- 300 grams (10 oz) or Arborio rice
- 200 grams (7 oz) of drained petit pois
- A large onion
- 4 cloves of garlic
- 600 ml (a pint) of chicken stock
- A dash of tomato puree
- A tablespoon of extra virgin olive oil
- Salt and pepper

Serves 4

Preparation

Peel and chop the onion thinly.

Peel and crush the garlic.

Put the extra virgin olive oil into your pressure cooker and heat it on medium fire.

Add the onion and garlic and sauté for about 10 minutes.

Add the Arborio rice and keep stirring it into the sauté for about 1 to 2 minutes.

Add the stock, season and stir.

Add the petit pois, the tomato puree and stir.

Seal the pressure cooker and cook for about 15 minutes.

Remove the lid and keep cooking, stirring continuously, until the stock has been fully absorbed by the rice before serving.

Recipe 5 – Spicy Lentils

Did you know that lentils were the staple food for most of mankind for millennia? This is because they are super rich in proteins (more than in meat in fact) and are also packed with those all essential micronutrients. They are also very filling, so they are excellent if you want to lose weight.

Ingredients

- 400 grams (13 oz) of dry green lentils
- A large onion
- 250 grams (8 oz) of chopped tomatoes
- 5 cloves of garlic
- A large carrot
- 10 bay leaves
- 2 red chili peppers
- Herbs de Provence or Italian herb seasoning
- 600 ml (a pint) of vegetable stock

- A tablespoon of extra virgin olive oil

- Salt and pepper

Serves 4 as a main or 8 as a side dish

Preparation

Soak the lentils in water for two hours.

Peel and chop the onion very finely.

Peel and slice the carrot (1/2 cm thick or 1/5 of an inch).

Peel and crush the garlic.

Put the olive oil into your pressure cooker and heat on medium fire.

Add the bay leaves, the carrot, the onion and the garlic and sauté for about 10 minutes.

In the meantime, drain the lentils, and prepare the chili peppers by cutting them in the middle, removing the seeds and chopping them thinly.

Add the lentils, the chili and the herbs.

Add the stock, season, stir and seal the pressure cooker.

Cook for 25 minutes before serving.

Recipe 6 – Steak Casserole

You can eat meat if you want to lose weight, as long as it is lean and it is not fried; here is a simple recipe for you.

Ingredients

- 400 grams (13 oz) of lean beef steak
- 2 large onions
- 2 large carrots
- 6 cloves of garlic
- 250 grams (8 oz) of chopped tomatoes
- 400 grams (13 oz) of potatoes
- 200 grams (7 oz) of parsnips
- A tablespoon of extra virgin olive oil
- A sprig of rosemary
- 10 bay leaves
- Salt and pepper

Serves 4

Preparation

Trim the fat from the stake and cut it into 2 cm (or one inch) pieces.

Peel and chop the onion roughly.

Peel and slice the garlic.

Peel and slice the carrots (1 cm thick or ½ inch).

Peel and cut the potatoes into big cubes (5 cm or 2 inches in size).

Wash and the parsnips (into slices about 1 inch or 2.5 cm thick).

Put the oil into the pressure cooker and heat on medium fire.

Add the onion, the bay leaves and the garlic and sauté for about 10 minutes.

In the meantime, remove the leaves from the rosemary.

Add the steak and the rosemary and cook for 2 minutes stirring continuously.

Add the chopped tomatoes, the potatoes, the parsnips and the stock; season and stir.

Seal the pressure cooker and cook for 30 minutes before serving.

Recipe 7 – Colombian Chicken Stew

If you like chicken, you can still eat it, as long as you choose lean cuts; so here is a recipe from South America which you can cook with your pressure cooker.

Ingredients

- 500 grams (16 oz) of lean white chicken meat
- 350 grams (12 oz) of potatoes
- 200 grams (7 oz) of tomatoes
- 300 grams (10 oz) of chicken stock
- 8 bay leaves
- Salt and pepper

Serves 4

Preparation

Trim any excess fat off the meat.

Peel the potatoes and cut them into wedges.

Wash and cut the tomatoes into large slices.

Put the chicken, the tomatoes, the bay leaves and the stock into the pressure cooker.

Seal and cook for 20 minutes before serving.

Recipe 8 – Corn Soup

Corn has really few calories, so this soup is excellent if you want to lose weight.

Ingredients

- 400 grams of corn
- 300 grams (10 oz) of potatoes
- A large onion
- A bunch of chives
- 3 garlic cloves
- A tablespoon (20 ml) of extra virgin olive oil
- 600 ml (1 pint) of vegetable stock
- Salt and pepper

Serves 4

Preparation

Peel and cut the onion.

Peel and crush the garlic.

Peel the potatoes and cut them into small cubes (2 cm or about 1 inch in size).

Put the extra virgin olive oil into the pressure cooker and heat on medium fire.

When the oil is sizzling, add the onion and garlic, stir and sauté for about 10 minutes.

Add the corn and the potatoes.

Add the stock, season and stir.

Seal the pressure cooker then cook for 15 minutes.

In the meantime, wash and chop the chives.

Remove the lid from the pressure cooker and blend the soup with a blender.

Cook for 2 more minutes, add the chives and serve.

Recipe 9 – Columbian Vegetable Soup

This soup is rich in micronutrients, and it has a very low calorie content; because the potatoes in the soup will release the starch, it will become thick and creamy without the need for you to add any fattening dairy products.

Ingredients

- 250 grams (8 oz) of fava beans
- 250 grams (8 oz) of garden peas
- 250 grams (8 oz) of potatoes
- 150 grams (5 oz) of corn
- A large onion
- 600 ml (1 pint) of vegetable stock
- A small bunch of parsley
- 1 tablespoon (20 ml) of extra virgin olive oil
- Salt and pepper

Serves 4

Preparation

Peel and chop the onion finely.

Put the olive oil into the pressure cooker and heat on medium fire.

Add the chopped onion and sauté for 10 minutes.

In the meantime, peel the potatoes and cut them into small cubes (1 cm or ½ inch in size).

Add the stock and season.

Add the fava beans, the garden peas, the cubed potatoes and the garden peas and stir.

Seal the pressure cooker and cook for 20 minutes.

In the meantime, chop the parsley.

Remove the lid from the pressure cooker, add the parsley and cook for another minute before serving.

Recipe 10 – Chicken and Black Bean Stew

Filling and very rich in protein, this dish is a variation on a pork dish, but with much less fat and calorie content.

Ingredients

- 450 grams (15 oz) of lean chicken
- 400 grams (13 oz) of black beans
- 200 grams (13 oz) of potatoes
- A large onion
- 3 garlic cloves
- 200 ml (7 oz) of chicken stock
- 150 ml (5 oz) of vegetable stock
- A chili pepper
- 1 tablespoon (20 ml) of extra virgin olive oil
- Salt and pepper

Serves 4

Preparation

Trim any excess fat from the chicken meat.

Drain the beans.

Peel and chop the onion finely.

Peel and slice the garlic.

Put the olive oil into the pressure cooker and heat on medium fire.

When the oil is sizzling, add the onion and garlic and sauté for 10 minutes.

In the meantime, peel the potatoes and chop them into large cubes (2 inches or about 5 cm in size).

Prepare the chili pepper; cut it in the middle and remove the seeds, then chop it finely.

Add the bay leaves, the beans, the potatoes, the vegetable and chicken stock and the chili pepper.

Season, stir, seal the pressure cooker and cook for 20 minutes before serving.

Recipe 11 – Chicken Curry with Eggplant and Squash

If you like curry, here is a lean curry dish for you.

Ingredients

- 400 grams (13 oz) of lean chicken meat
- 300 grams (10 oz) of eggplant
- 300 grams of squash
- A large onion
- 6 cloves of garlic
- A carrot
- 300 ml (1/2 pint) of chicken stock
- Curry paste as necessary (1 to 3 tablespoons to taste)
- 2 chili peppers
- A few mint leaves
- A small bunch of parsley

- A small bunch of coriander
- A tablespoon (20 ml) of extra virgin olive oil
- Salt and pepper

Serves 4

Preparation

Peel and chop the onion roughly.

Peel and slice the garlic.

Peel and cut the carrot into small pieces.

Cut the chili peppers in two, remove the seeds and chop them finely.

Wash and cut the eggplant into cubes (2 inches or about 5 cm in size).

Wash and cut the squash into cubes (2 inches or about 5 cm in size).

Chop the coriander.

Put the olive oil into the pressure cooker and heat on medium fire.

Add the onion, the carrot, the garlic and the chili peppers and sauté for 19 minutes.

Add the curry paste and mix well.

Add the chicken and cook for 5 minutes.

Add the stock and the chopped coriander, season, seal the pressure cooker and cook for 10 minutes.

Let the pressure cooker cool, remove the lid and add the squash and the eggplant.

Stir and seal the pressure cooker; then cook for another 15 minutes.

In the meantime, chop the parsley.

Add the parsley and mint to the curry, cook for another minute and serve.

Recipe 12 – Vietnamese Chicken Noodle Soup

Here is a very tasty and exotic soup which has a low calorie intake and is very good for your diet.

Ingredients

- 4 chicken drumsticks
- 300 grams (10 oz) of rice noodles
- A large onion
- 300 ml (1/2 pint) of vegetable stock.
- 300 ml (1/2 pint) of chicken stock.
- A chili pepper
- A bunch of spring onions
- A bunch of dill
- A bunch of parsley
- Salt and pepper

Serves 4

Preparation

Peel and cut the onion into thin rounds.

Put the vegetable stock, the chicken stock, the onion and the chicken into your pressure cooker.

Season and seal the pressure cooker.

Cook for 20 minutes.

In the meantime, chop the parsley, the dill and the spring onions.

Cut the chili pepper in the middle, remove the seeds and chop it thinly.

Let the pressure cooker cool, remove the lid, add the parsley, the dill, the spring onions, the noodles and the chili.

Cook for 5 more minutes without the lid before serving.

Recipe 13 – Wild Mushroom Risotto

If you cook risotto with a normal sauce pan, you need to keep stirring and adding the stock a bit a time, but if you do it with the pressure cooker, it is much faster. Risotto is quite filling and fairly low in calories, so it is good if you want to lose weight.

Ingredients

- 60 grams (2 oz) of dried wild mushrooms
- 300 grams (10 oz) of Arborio rice
- 3 cloves of garlic
- 450 ml (15 oz) of chicken stock
- A dash of tomato puree
- A small bunch of parsley
- 1 tablespoon (20 ml) of extra virgin olive oil
- Salt and pepper

Serves 4

Preparation

Soak the mushrooms in warm water for 15 minutes.

Peel and crush the garlic.

Put the olive oil into the pressure cooker and heat on medium fire.

Add the Arborio rice and the crushed garlic and keep cooking while stirring continuously for 2 minutes.

Add the mushrooms and cook for another 2 minutes stirring continuously.

Add the stock and a dash of tomato puree.

Season and stir, then seal the pressure cooker and cook for 15 minutes.

In the meantime, chop the parsley.

Let the pressure cooker cool, add the parsley and cook for another 3 to 5 minutes, until the stock has been fully absorbed by the rice before serving.

Recipe 14 – Potato and Leek Soup

This traditional British soup is very good to fill you up, keep you lean and has quite a lot of flavor.

Ingredients

- 400 grams (13 oz) of leek
- 300 grams (10 oz) of potatoes
- 1 large onion
- 4 cloves of garlic
- 600 ml (1 pint) of chicken stock
- A bunch of parsley
- 1 tablespoon (20 ml) of extra virgin olive oil
- Salt and pepper

Serves 4

Preparation

Peel and chop the onion finely.

Peel and crush the garlic.

Put the olive oil into the pressure cooker and heat on medium fire.

Add the onion and garlic and sauté for 10 minutes.

In the meantime, wash and chop the leek and peel and cut the potatoes into cubes (1 inch or about 2.5 cm in size).

Add the stock and season.

Add the leak and cubed potatoes.

Stir and seal the pressure cooker.

Cook for 20 minutes.

In the meantime, chop the parsley.

Let the pressure cooker cool, remove the lid and add blend with a blender.

Add the parsley and cook for another minute before serving.

Recipe 15 – Salmon Fillet

When we are talking about proteins, you should know that fish proteins are much healthier than meat proteins, what is more, fat fish, like salmon, is a bit like some fat vegetables; despite being fat, it makes you slim down, as a research on Inuit diet shows. Here is a very simple way of cooking salmon fillet.

Ingredients

- 4 salmon fillets, boned and scaled
- A large onion
- A carrot
- 3 cloves of garlic
- 10 bay leaves
- A bunch of dill
- 600 ml (1 pint) of vegetable stock
- A lemon
- A bowl of mustard

- A bowl of mayonnaise
- Salt and pepper

Serves 4

Preparation

Peel the onion, the garlic and the carrot.

Chop the dill finely.

Put the salmon fillets at the bottom of your pressure cooker.

Add the stock and season.

Add the onion, the carrot, the garlic, the bay leaves to the stock.

Add the chopped dill.

Seal the pressure cooker and cook for 15 minutes.

Allow the pressure cooker to cool and remove the lid.

Remove the salmon fillet and drain the, before serving them with a bowl of mustard, a lemon and a bowl of mayonnaise.

Recipe 16 – Seafood Chowder

Seafood is lean and rich in antioxidants, so you really need to try this chowder which you can easily prepare with your pressure cooker.

Ingredients

- 400 grams (13 oz) of fish (you can choose your favourites)
- A large onion
- 300 grams (10 oz) potatoes
- 300 ml (10 oz) of semi skimmed milk
- 450 ml (15 oz) of chicken stock
- 300 ml (10 oz) of vegetable stock
- Salt and pepper

Serves 4

Preparation

Cut the fish into small chunks.

Peel and cut the potatoes into small cubes (1 inch or 2.5 cm in size).

Peel and chop the onion finely.

Put the onion, the potatoes, the fish and the stock in your pressure cooker.

Add the milk, season and stir.

Put the lid on the pressure cooker and cook for 20 minutes.

Allow the pressure cooker to cool, remove the lid and cook for another 5 minutes before serving.

Recipe 17 – Rabbit Casserole

If you want to lose weight, you can still eat meat, but you need to choose very lean meat; rabbit is very, very lean and it is absolutely delicious.

Ingredients

- 500 grams (17 oz) of rabbit, cut into pieces
- 300 grams (10 oz) of potatoes
- 200 grams (7 oz) of dried green lentils
- 300 ml (1/2 pint) of chicken stock
- A large onion
- A medium carrot
- A stalk of celery
- 10 bay leaves
- 3 cloves of garlic
- A tablespoon (20 ml) of extra virgin olive oil

- A few leaves of fresh sage

- A teaspoon (5 grams) of dried thyme

- Salt and pepper

Serves 4

Preparation

Soak the lentils in water for 2 hours.

Peel and chop the onion finely.

Peel and crush the garlic.

Cut the celery into very small bits.

Peel and cut the carrot into very small bits.

Put the oil in your pressure cooker and heat on medium fire.

Add the bay leaves, the onion, the garlic, the celery and the carrot to the oil, stir and sauté for 10 minutes.

Add the rabbit and cook for another 5 minutes.

In the meantime, drain the lentils.

Add the potatoes and the lentils.

Add the stock, the sage leaves and the thyme, season and stir.

Cook for 30 minutes before serving.

Recipe 18 – Passata di Verdura

This recipe is a variation on minestrone; unlike it, though, it is much thicker and the vegetables are blended, which makes it ideal if you have children as they tend to prefer it this way.

Ingredients

- 300 grams (10 oz) of cannellini beans
- A medium sized courgette
- 100 grams (3 oz) of long grain rice
- A large onion
- A stalk of celery
- 300 grams (10 oz) of potatoes
- A large carrot
- 3 cloves of garlic
- A tablespoon (20 ml) of extra virgin olive oil
- 600 ml (20 oz) of chicken stock
- 300 ml (10 oz) of vegetable stock
- A small sprig of parsley
- Salt and pepper

Serves 4

Preparation

Wash and slice the courgette (into 1 cm slices).

Peel and chop the onion roughly.

Peel and slice the garlic cloves.

Rinse the cannellini beans.

Peel and cut the potatoes into small cubes (2 cm or 1 inch in size).

Wash and chop the celery stalk.

Peel and cut the carrot into slices (1 cm or ½ inch thick).

Put the onion, the garlic, the celery and the carrot into your pressure cooker.

Add the extra virgin olive oil and sauté for about 10 minutes.

Add the cannellini beans, the potatoes and the courgettes.

Add the chicken stock and the vegetable stock.

Season and seal the pressure cooker.

Cook for 15 minutes.

Allow the pressure cooker to cool, remove the lid, whizz it with a blender until it is smooth and thick and add the rice.

Seal the pressure cooker again and cook for another 10 minutes.

Chop the parsley and garnish the minestrone before serving.

Recipe 19 – Classical Milanese Risotto

Did you know that in Milan they eat much more risotto than pasta? This is a classical dish from the foggy city, which was allegedly discovered when making the stained glass for its glorious cathedral.

Ingredients

- 1 gram of saffron
- 300 grams (10 oz) of Arborio rice
- 3 cloves of garlic
- 450 ml (15 oz) of chicken stock
- 1 tablespoon (20 ml) of extra virgin olive oil
- Salt and pepper

Serves 4

Preparation

Peel and crush the garlic.

Put the olive oil into the pressure cooker and heat on medium fire.

Add the Arborio rice and the crushed garlic and keep cooking while stirring continuously for 2 minutes.

Add the saffron and cook for another 1 minute stirring continuously.

Add the stock and a dash of tomato puree.

Season and stir, then seal the pressure cooker and cook for 15 minutes.

Let the pressure cooker cool, add the parsley and cook for another 3 to 5 minutes, until the stock has been fully absorbed by the rice before serving.

Recipe 20 – Smoked Haddock Fillet

Ingredients

- 4 salmon fillets, boned and scaled
- A large onion
- A carrot
- 3 cloves of garlic
- A bunch of spring onions
- 10 bay leaves
- A chili pepper
- A bunch of thyme
- 600 ml (1 pint) of vegetable stock
- A lemon
- A bowl of mustard
- A bowl of tartar sauce
- Salt and pepper

Serves 4

Preparation

Peel the onion, the garlic and the carrot.

Chop the thyme finely.

Wash and cut the spring onions.

Put the smoked haddock fillets at the bottom of your pressure cooker.

Add the stock and season.

Add the onion, the carrot, the garlic, the chilli (whole) the bay leaves to the stock.

Add the thyme and the spring onions.

Seal the pressure cooker and cook for 15 minutes.

Allow the pressure cooker to cool and remove the lid.

Remove the smoked haddock fillets and drain the haddock fillets and reduce the stock to 1/3 before serving with a bowl of mustard, a lemon and a bowl of tartar sauce.

Recipe 21 – Spinach Soup with Rice

Ingredients

- 600 grams (20 oz) of spinach
- 300 grams (10 oz) of potatoes
- 100 grams (3 oz) of long grain rice
- A medium carrot
- 1 large onion
- 4 cloves of garlic
- 600 ml (1 pint) of chicken stock
- 1 tablespoon (20 ml) of extra virgin olive oil
- Salt and pepper

Serves 4

Preparation

Peel and chop the onion finely.

Peel and chop the carrot finely.

Peel and crush the garlic.

Put the olive oil into the pressure cooker and heat on medium fire.

Add the onion, the carrot and garlic and sauté for 10 minutes.

In the meantime, wash the spinach and peel and cut the potatoes into cubes (1 inch or about 2.5 cm in size).

Add the stock and season.

Add the spinach, the rice and cubed potatoes.

Stir and seal the pressure cooker.

Cook for 20 minutes.

Let the pressure cooker cool, remove the lid and add blend with a blender.

Cook for another minute before serving.

Recipe 22 – Leftover Chicken Chowder

Here is another leftover chicken recipe which you can use to save money and lose weight.

Ingredients

- 350 grams (12 oz) of leftover chicken
- A large onion
- A shallot
- A bunch of spring onions
- 2 cloves of garlic
- 350 grams (12 oz) potatoes
- 300 ml (10 oz) of semi skimmed milk
- 450 ml (15 oz) of chicken stock
- 300 ml (10 oz) of vegetable stock
- A bunch of coriander
- Salt and pepper

Serves 4

Preparation

Remove any bones from the chicken and cut it into small chunks.

Peel and cut the potatoes into small cubes (1 inch or 2.5 cm in size).

Peel and chop the shallot finely.

Peel and chop the onion finely.

Wash and chop the spring onions.

Put the onion, the spring onions, the shallot, the potatoes, the chicken and the stock in your pressure cooker.

Add the milk, season and stir.

Put the lid on the pressure cooker and cook for 20 minutes.

In the meantime, chop the coriander.

Allow the pressure cooker to cool, remove the lid, add the coriander, stir and cook for another 5 minutes before serving.

Recipe 23 – Root Vegetable Stew

Root vegetables are quite filling, but they contain few calories; here is a wonderful and tasty stew for cold evenings.

Ingredients

- 200 grams (7 oz) of parsnip
- 200 grams (7 oz) of potatoes
- 200 grams (7 oz) of beet
- 100 grams (3 oz) of rutabaga
- 100 grams (3 oz) of turnip
- 3 medium carrots
- 2 large onions
- 4 cloves of garlic
- 12 bay leaves
- 450 ml (15 oz) of vegetable stock

- A teaspoon (5 grams) of dry sage
- A teaspoon (5 grams) of dry thyme
- A teaspoon (5 grams) of dry rosemary
- A tablespoon of extra virgin olive oil
- Salt and pepper

Serves 4

Preparation

Peel and slice the onion roughly.

Peel and crush the garlic.

Put the olive oil in the pressure cooker and heat on medium fire.

Add the onion and garlic when the oil is sizzling and sauté for 10 minutes.

In the meantime, peel and slice the carrots (1 cm or ½ inch thick).

Peel and cut the root vegetables into small cubes (2 cm or 1 inch in size).

Add the root vegetables and cover with the stock.

Season, add the dry thyme, the dry sage and the dry rosemary.

Stir and seal the pressure cooker.

Cook for 25 minutes.

Allow the pressure cooker to cool and remove the lead, then cook for another 5 to 10 minutes, until most of the liquid has been absorbed, before serving.

Recipe 24 – Chicken in Spicy Tomato Sauce

Here is a simple chicken recipe which is good for your weight loss and very tasty.

Ingredients

- 400 grams (13 oz) of chicken breasts
- 250 grams (8 oz) of chopped tomatoes
- A few basil leaves
- A large onion
- 4 cloves of garlic
- 300 ml (1/2 pint) of chicken stock
- A teaspoon (5 grams) of tarragon (optional, if you like a bitter taste)
- A chili pepper
- A tablespoon (20 grams) of dry oregano
- A tablespoon (20 ml) of extra virgin olive oil
- Salt and pepper

Serves 4

Preparation

Peel and chop the onion fairly finely.

Peel and crush the garlic.

Put the extra virgin olive oil in your pressure cooker and heat on medium fire.

In the meantime, cut the chilli in two and remove the seeds.

Chop the chilli very finely.

Add the chilli and the chicken and stir well; cook for 10 minutes.

Add the tomatoes, the basil leaves, the oregano and the tarragon.

Stir and add the chicken stock.

Seal the pressure cooker and cook for 20 minutes.

Allow the pressure cooker to cool; remove the lid and cook for another 5-10 minutes, until the sauce is thick, before serving.

Recipe 25 – Trout Fillets

Trout must be everybody's favorite freshwater fish; it is usually cheaper than salt water fish, but it is as nutritious and lean, especially if it is wild.

Ingredients

- 4 salmon fillets, boned and scaled
- A large onion
- A carrot
- 6 cloves of garlic
- 12 bay leaves
- A chili pepper
- A bunch of dill
- A bunch of thyme
- 600 ml (1 pint) of vegetable stock
- A lime

- A bowl of tartar sauce
- A bowl of mayonnaise
- Salt and pepper

Serves 4

Preparation

Peel the onion, the garlic and the carrot.

Chop the dill and the thyme finely.

Put the trout fillets at the bottom of your pressure cooker.

Add the stock and season.

Add the onion, the carrot, the garlic, the chilli and the bay leaves to the stock.

Add the chopped dill and thyme.

Seal the pressure cooker and cook for 15 minutes.

Allow the pressure cooker to cool and remove the lid.

Remove the trout fillet and drain the, before serving them with a bowl of tartar sauce, a slice of lime and a bowl of mayonnaise

Recipe 26 – Risotto and Asparagus

Asparagus is a special vegetable because it actually uses more energy to be digested than it gives us, thus, it is ideal if you want to lose weight.

Ingredients

- 180 grams (6 oz) of asparagus
- 300 grams (10 oz) of Arborio rice
- 3 cloves of garlic
- 450 ml (15 oz) of chicken stock
- A dash of tomato puree
- A small bunch of parsley
- 1 tablespoon (20 ml) of extra virgin olive oil
- Salt and pepper

Serves 4

Preparation

Slice the asparagus (about 5 cm long or about 2 inches).

Peel and crush the garlic.

Put the olive oil into the pressure cooker and heat on medium fire.

Add the Arborio rice and the crushed garlic and keep cooking while stirring continuously for 2 minutes.

Add the asparagus and cook for another 2 minutes stirring continuously.

Add the stock and a dash of tomato puree.

Season and stir, then seal the pressure cooker and cook for 15 minutes.

In the meantime, chop the parsley.

Let the pressure cooker cool, add the parsley and cook for another 3 to 5 minutes, until the stock has been fully absorbed by the rice before serving.

Recipe 27 – Pheasant and Mushroom Stew

Pheasant, if caught from the wild, is an excellent bird to eat as it is very tasty and very lean. Here is a great recipe you can cook with your pressure cooker.

Ingredients

- A large pheasant, cut into pieces
- 3 large onions
- 180 grams (6 oz) of chestnut mushrooms
- 60 grams (2 oz) of dry wild mushrooms
- 300 ml (1/2 a pint) of chicken stock
- 2 medium carrots
- A stalk of celery
- 6 garlic cloves
- A glass of red wine
- A nutmeg

- 6 bay leaves
- A chili pepper
- Salt and pepper

Serves 4

Preparation

Soak the wild mushrooms in warm water for 10 minutes.

Peel and slice the onion roughly.

Peel and chop the carrot thinly.

Cut the celery into small pieces.

Peel and crush the garlic.

Put the olive oil in your pressure cooker and heat on medium fire.

When the oil is hot, add the onion, the carrot, the celery and the garlic and sauté for 10 minutes.

In the meantime, slice the chestnut mushrooms.

Add the pheasant.

Grate the nutmeg on the pheasant and stir.

Add the glass of wine.

Cook for another 5 minutes.

Add the wild and chestnut mushrooms.

Add the bay leaves and the stock.

Season, stir gently and seal the pressure cooker.

Cook for 30 minutes.

Remove the lid after you have cooled down the cooker and cook for another 10 minutes without the lid before serving.

Recipe 28 – Chicken Casserole

Chicken is a fairly lean meat, especially if you buy rooster chicken; here is a great casserole you can cook with your pressure cooker.

Ingredients

- 600 grams (20 oz) of chicken meat, cut into pieces
- 300 grams (10 oz) of potatoes
- 200 grams (7 oz) of garden peas
- 300 ml (1/2 pint) of chicken stock
- A large onion
- A medium carrot
- A stalk of celery
- A small bunch pf parsley
- 10 bay leaves
- A chili pepper

- 3 cloves of garlic
- A tablespoon (20 ml) of extra virgin olive oil
- A few leaves of fresh sage
- A teaspoon (5 grams) of dried rosemary
- Salt and pepper

Serves 4

Preparation

Peel and chop the onion finely.

Peel and crush the garlic.

Cut the chilli in the middle, remove the seeds and chop finely.

Cut the celery into very small bits.

Peel and cut the carrot into very small bits.

Put the oil in your pressure cooker and heat on medium fire.

Add the bay leaves, the onion, the garlic, the celery, the carrot and the chilli pepper to the oil, stir and sauté for 10 minutes.

Add the chicken and cook for another 5 minutes.

Add the potatoes and the garden peas.

Add the stock, the sage leaves and the rosemary, season and stir.

Cook for 30 minutes.

In the meantime, chop the parsley.

Allow the pressure cooker to cool, remove the lid, add the chopped parsley and cook for another minute before serving.

Recipe 29 – Peas and Beans Soup

This soup is very rich in proteins and very poor in fats, which means that it will keep you full for long and you will not find yourself snacking between meals.

Ingredients

- 300 grams (10 oz) of mixed beans
- 150 grams (5 oz) of garden peas
- A medium carrot
- 150 grams (5 oz) of potatoes
- 1 large onion
- 4 cloves of garlic
- 600 ml (1 pint) of chicken stock
- A bunch of dill
- 1 tablespoon (20 ml) of extra virgin olive oil
- Salt and pepper

Serves 4

Preparation

Peel and chop the onion finely.

Peel and crush the garlic.

Peel and chop the carrot finely.

Put the olive oil into the pressure cooker and heat on medium fire.

Add the onion, the chopped carrot and garlic and sauté for 10 minutes.

In the meantime, peel and cut the potatoes into cubes (1 inch or about 2.5 cm in size).

Add the stock and season.

Add the peas, the beans and cubed potatoes.

Stir and seal the pressure cooker.

Cook for 20 minutes.

In the meantime, chop the dill.

Let the pressure cooker cool, add the dill and cook for another minute before serving.

Recipe 30 – Chicken and Root Vegetable Stew

If you like your stews with a bit of meat, here is a perfect one for you.

Ingredients

- 8 chicken legs
- 120 grams (4 oz) of garden peas
- 100 grams (3 oz) of parsnip
- 100 grams (3 oz) of potatoes
- 100 grams (3 oz) of beet
- 60 grams (2 oz) of rutabaga
- 60 grams (2 oz) of turnip
- 2 medium carrots
- 2 large onions
- 5 cloves of garlic
- 12 bay leaves
- 300 ml (10 oz) of chicken stock
- 150 ml (5 oz) of vegetable stock
- A teaspoon (5 grams) of dry sage
- A teaspoon (5 grams) of dry thyme
- A teaspoon (5 grams) of dry rosemary
- A tablespoon of extra virgin olive oil
- Salt and pepper

Serves 4

Preparation

Peel and slice the onion roughly.

Peel and crush the garlic.

Put the olive oil in the pressure cooker and heat on medium fire.

Add the onion and garlic when the oil is sizzling and sauté for 10 minutes.

In the meantime, peel and slice the carrots (1 cm or ½ inch thick).

Peel and cut the root vegetables into small cubes (2 cm or 1 inch in size).

Add the chicken and cook for another 5 minutes, stirring continuously.

Add the vegetables and cover with the stock.

Season, add the dry thyme, the dry sage and the dry rosemary.

Stir and seal the pressure cooker.

Cook for 25 minutes.

Allow the pressure cooker to cool and remove the lead, then cook for another 5 to 10 minutes, until most of the liquid has been absorbed, before serving.

Recipe 31 – Wild Mushroom Soup

Earthy and comforting, this is a great soup with low calories for autumn and winter days.

Ingredients

- 60 grams (2 oz) of dry wild mushrooms
- 200 grams (7 oz) of chestnut mushrooms
- 250 grams (8 oz) of potatoes
- 3 cloves of garlic
- 200 ml (a cup) of semi skimmed milk
- A tablespoon (20 grams) of plain flour
- 600 ml (1 pint) of vegetable stock
- A small bunch of parsley
- A tablespoon (20 ml) of extra virgin olive oil
- Salt and pepper

Serves 4

Preparation

Soak the wild mushrooms in a bowl of warm water for 10 minutes.

Peel and crush the garlic.

Slice the chestnut mushrooms.

Peel and cut the potatoes into small cubes (1 cm or ½ inch in size).

Put the olive oil into the pressure cooker and heat on medium fire.

Add the mushrooms and the garlic and sauté for 5 minutes, stirring regularly.

Add the flour and incorporate it into the mushrooms gently.

Add the milk and cook for another 3 minutes.

Add the stock and the potatoes.

Season and stir.

Put the lid on the pressure cooker and cook for 25 minutes.

In the meantime, chop the parsley.

Let the pressure cooker cool and remove the lid.

Add the parsley and cook for 2 more minutes before serving.

Recipe 32 – Clam Chowder

Here is a super-delicious and super healthy chowder which will give you the flavors of the sea and very few calories.

Ingredients

- 300 grams (10 oz) of clams
- A large onion
- A shallot
- A bunch of spring onions
- 3 cloves of garlic
- A chili pepper
- A small ginger bulb
- 300 grams (10 oz) potatoes
- 300 ml (10 oz) of semi skimmed milk
- 450 ml (15 oz) of chicken stock

- 300 ml (10 oz) of vegetable stock
- A bunch of chives
- Salt and pepper

Serves 4

Preparation

Rinse the clams with cold water and drain them.

Peel and cut the potatoes into small cubes (1 inch or 2.5 cm in size).

Peel and chop the shallot finely.

Peel and chop the onion finely.

Chop the chives.

Peel and slice the ginger bulb.

Wash and chop the spring onions.

Put the onion, the spring onions, the shallot, the potatoes, the clams, the chilli, the ginger and the stock in your pressure cooker.

Add the milk, season and stir.

Put the lid on the pressure cooker and cook for 20 minutes.

In the meantime, chop the chives roughly.

Let the pressure cooker cool, remove the lid, add the chives, stir and cook for another 5 minutes before serving.

Recipe 33 – Aromatic Rabbit Casserole

Lean and full of flavor, rabbit should be your favorite meat when it comes to losing weight. Here is a special casserole for you.

Ingredients

- 500 grams of rabbit meat, cut into pieces
- 2 large onions
- 4 cloves of garlic
- 300 grams (10 oz) of garden peas
- A stalk of celery
- A medium carrot
- A glass of white wine
- A nutmeg
- A chili pepper
- A tablespoon (20 grams) of dry thyme
- A tablespoon (20 grams) of plain flour
- 150 ml (5 oz) of semi skimmed milk
- 150 ml (5 oz) of chicken stock
- A tablespoon (20 ml) of extra virgin olive oil
- Salt and pepper

Serves 4

Preparation

Peel and chop the onions very finely.

Peel and crush the garlic.

Cut the celery stalk into very small pieces.

Peel and cut the onion into very small pieces.

Put the oil in your pressure cooker and heat on medium fire.

When the oil is hot, add the onion, the garlic, the celery and the carrot.

Sauté for 10 minutes.

Add the rabbit and stir.

Add the white wine and grate the nutmeg on the rabbit, stir and cook for another 5 minutes.

Add the flour and stir.

Add the milk and cook for another 3 minutes.

Add the thyme, the stock, the peas and season.

Stir and seal the pressure cooker.

Cook for 35 minutes before serving.

Recipe 34 – Pea and Ham Soup

Ingredients

- 120 grams (4 oz) of lean ham, in one slice
- 300 grams (10 oz) of peas
- 300 grams (10 oz) of potatoes
- 1 large onion
- 4 cloves of garlic
- 300 ml (1/2 pint) of chicken stock
- 300 ml (1/2 pint) of vegetable stock
- 1 tablespoon (20 ml) of extra virgin olive oil
- Salt and pepper

Serves 4

Preparation

Cut the ham into small squares.

Peel and chop the onion finely.

Peel and crush the garlic.

Put the olive oil into the pressure cooker and heat on medium fire.

Add the onion and garlic and sauté for 10 minutes.

In the meantime, peel and cut the potatoes into cubes (1 inch or about 2.5 cm in size).

Add the stock and season.

Add the peas and cubed potatoes.

Stir and seal the pressure cooker.

Cook for 20 minutes.

Let the pressure cooker cool, remove the lid and add blend with a blender.

Add the ham and cook for another minute before serving.

Recipe 35 – Steamed Spring Vegetables

What's sweeter and healthier than spring vegetables? Here is how you can cook them in literally 5 minutes using your pressure cooker.

Ingredients

- 120 grams (4 oz) of baby asparagus
- 120 grams (4 oz) of pea pods
- 120 grams (4 oz) of baby chard
- 120 grams (4 oz) of fava beans
- 120 grams (4 oz) of spring onions
- 120 grams (4 oz) of baby carrots
- 120 grams (4 oz) of baby courgettes
- 1/2 cup (100 ml) of vegetable stock
- A bunch of chives
- Salt (and pepper if you want)

Serves 4

Preparation

Wash all the vegetables.

Cut the baby courgettes in two lengthways.

Chop the spring onions coarsely.

Chop the chives thinly.

Put all the vegetables in your pressure cooker.

Add the chives and the stock.

Season, stir and place the lid on your pressure cooker.

Heat on high fire for 5 minutes before serving.

Recipe 36 – Game and Wild Mushroom Casserole

Game meat is always leaner than other types of meat; this is because the animals are free to roam around and enjoy their lives, burning *their* fat before you consume it. This is the perfect casserole for a Sunday meal.

Ingredients

- 500 grams (17 oz) of game, cut into bite size pieces
- 300 grams (10 oz) of potatoes
- 100 grams (3 oz) of dried wild mushrooms
- 300 ml (1/2 pint) of chicken stock
- A large onion
- A medium carrot
- A stalk of celery
- 10 bay leaves
- 3 cloves of garlic

- A glass of red wine

- A tablespoon (20 ml) of extra virgin olive oil

- A few leaves of fresh sage

- A teaspoon (5 grams) of dried thyme

- A teaspoon (5 grams) of dried rosemary

- Salt and pepper

Serves 4

Preparation

Soak the wild mushrooms in warm water for 15 minutes.

Peel and chop the onion finely.

Peel and crush the garlic.

Cut the celery into very small bits.

Peel and cut the carrot into very small bits.

Put the oil in your pressure cooker and heat on medium fire.

Add the bay leaves, the onion, the garlic, the celery and the carrot to the oil, stir and sauté for 10 minutes.

Add the game meat and cook for another 5 minutes.

Add the glass of wine and cook for 3 more minutes.

In the meantime, drain the wild mushrooms.

Add the potatoes and the mushrooms.

Add the stock, the sage leaves and the thyme, the rosemary, season and stir.

Cook for 30 minutes before serving.

Recipe 37 – Risotto and Courgettes

Here is another delicious and healthy risotto dish from northern Italy which you can prepare easily and quickly with your pressure cooker.

Ingredients

- 2 medium courgettes
- 300 grams (10 oz) of Arborio rice
- 3 cloves of garlic
- 450 ml (15 oz) of chicken stock
- A dash of tomato puree
- A small bunch of parsley
- 1 tablespoon (20 ml) of extra virgin olive oil
- Salt and pepper

Serves 4

Preparation

Wash and slice the courgettes (1/2 cm thick, or about 1/5 of an inch).

Peel and crush the garlic.

Put the olive oil into the pressure cooker and heat on medium fire.

Add the Arborio rice and the crushed garlic and keep cooking while stirring continuously for 2 minutes.

Add the courgettes and cook for another minute stirring continuously.

Add the stock and a dash of tomato puree.

Season and stir, then seal the pressure cooker and cook for 15 minutes.

In the meantime, chop the parsley.

Let the pressure cooker cool, add the parsley and cook for another 3 to 5 minutes, until the stock has been fully absorbed by the rice before serving.

Recipe 38 – Artichoke and Anchovy Stew

Thus dish is particularly indicated if you feel a bit tired; this is usually a sign that you need iron, and with the added omega oil from the anchovies, you will be back on your feet in no time at all!

Ingredients

- 300 grams (10 oz) of artichokes
- 250 grams (8 oz) of chopped tomatoes
- A bunch of spring onions
- 3 shallots
- 4 cloves of garlic
- A bunch of fresh flat leaf parsley
- 60 grams of anchovies
- A chili pepper
- A lemon
- A tablespoon (20 ml) of extra virgin olive oil
- Salt and pepper

Serves 4

Preparation

Cut the artichokes into bite size pieces, removing the fluffy core and any thorns.

Place the artichokes in a bowl of water and immediately add the juice of the lemon.

Peel and chop the shallots very finely.

Peel and crush the garlic.

Cut the chilli in the middle, remove the seeds and chop it thinly.

Put the olive oil in your pressure cooker and heat on medium fire.

When the oil is hot, add the shallots, the garlic, the anchovies and the chilli and sauté for 5 minutes.

Drain and add the artichokes.

Add the chopped tomatoes, season and stir.

Seal the pressure cooker and cook for 20 to 25 minutes.

In the meantime, chop the parsley.

Remove the lid once you have let the pressure cooker cool, add the parsley and cook for another 2 minutes before serving.

Recipe 39 – Halibut Fillet and Lemongrass

Here is a delicious and fresh dish which is so low in calories that you won't believe it!

Ingredients

- 4 halibut fillets, boned and scaled
- A large onion
- A carrot
- 5 cloves of garlic
- 8 bay leaves
- A bunch of dill
- A few mint leaves
- A bunch of thyme
- 4 lemongrass sticks
- A chili pepper

- A bunch of sprung onions
- 600 ml (1 pint) of vegetable stock
- A lemon
- A bowl of mustard
- A bowl of mayonnaise
- Salt and pepper

Serves 4

Preparation

Peel the onion, the garlic and the carrot.

Chop the dill and the thyme finely.

Chop the spring onions.

Put the halibut fillets at the bottom of your pressure cooker.

Add the stock and season.

Add the onion, the carrot, the garlic, the chilli the bay leaves to the stock.

Add the chopped dill and thyme.

Add the mint leaves and the lemongrass sticks.

Seal the pressure cooker and cook for 15 minutes.

Allow the pressure cooker to cool and remove the lid.

Remove the halibut fillet and drain the, before serving them with a bowl of mustard, a lemon and a bowl of mayonnaise

Recipe 40 – Turkey Breast and Fennel Stew

This is an easy stew to give flavor to your turkey; as we know, turkey can be a both flavorless and it can get a bit dry, but not with this low calorie pressure cooker recipe.

Ingredients

- 4 turkey breasts
- 4 fennel bulbs
- 5 garlic cloves
- A chili pepper
- A bunch of dill
- A glass of white wine
- 450 ml (15 oz) of vegetable stock
- 5 bay leaves
- Salt and pepper

Serves 4

Preparation

Cut the turkey breasts into bite size pieces.

Wash and slice the fennel bulbs (1 cm or ½ inch thick).

Cut the chilli in half, remove the seeds and chop it thinly.

Peel the garlic and slice it thinly.

Put the stock in your pressure cooker and heat it; do not put the lid on yet.

As the stock is boiling, add the chilli, the garlic and the fennel bulbs.

Seal the pressure cooker and cook for 15 minutes.

In the meantime, chop the dill very thinly.

Allow the pressure cooker to cool and remove the lid.

Add the turkey and the dill.

Add the white wine and cook without lid for another 3 minutes.

Season, stir and put the lid back on.

Cook for another 10 minutes before serving.

Recipe 41 – Chickpea Chowder

Chickpeas are an essential ingredient in all good diets; this is because they are very rich in proteins and have fairly low calorie content; what is more, they make you feel full very soon and for a very long time.

Ingredients

- 300 grams (10 oz) of chickpeas
- 150 grams (5 oz) of garden peas
- A medium carrot
- 120 grams (4 oz) of potatoes
- 1 large onion
- 3 cloves of garlic
- 600 ml (1 pint) of vegetable stock
- A bunch of parsley
- 1 tablespoon (20 ml) of extra virgin olive oil
- Salt and pepper

Serves 4

Preparation

Peel and chop the onion finely.

Peel and crush the garlic.

Peel and chop the carrot finely.

Put the olive oil into the pressure cooker and heat on medium fire.

Add the onion, the chopped carrot and garlic and sauté for 10 minutes.

In the meantime, peel and cut the potatoes into cubes (1 inch or about 2.5 cm in size).

Add the vegetable stock and season.

Add the chickpeas, the garden peas and cubed potatoes.

Stir and seal the pressure cooker.

Cook for 20 minutes.

In the meantime, chop the parsley.

Let the pressure cooker cool, add the parsley and cook for another minute before serving.

Recipe 42 – Spicy Sea Bass Fillet

Did you know that sea bass has less than 100 calories per 100 grams? Considering the average fillet is about 2-300 grams, you can easily work out how good it is to lose weight.

Ingredients

- 4 salmon fillets, boned and scaled
- A large onion
- A carrot
- 6 cloves of garlic
- 12 bay leaves
- A small ginger bulb
- 2 lemongrass sticks
- 3 chili peppers
- A bunch of thyme
- A few mint leaves

- 600 ml (1 pint) of vegetable stock

- A lemon

- A bowl of mustard

- A bowl of tartar sauce

- Salt and pepper

Serves 4

Preparation

Peel the onion, the garlic and the carrot.

Chop the thyme finely.

Peel and slice the ginger bulb.

Put the sea bass fillets at the bottom of your pressure cooker.

Add the stock and season.

Add the onion, the carrot, the garlic, the bay leaves to the stock.

Add the chopped thyme and the mint leaves.

Add the chilli peppers (as they are, do not cut them).

Add the lemongrass sticks and the ginger.

Seal the pressure cooker and cook for 15 minutes.

Allow the pressure cooker to cool and remove the lid.

Remove the sea bass fillet and drain the, before serving them with a bowl of mustard, a lemon and a bowl of tartar sauce.

Recipe 43 – Risotto and Leftover Chicken

If you have leftover chicken meat, do not waste it; instead use it to cook this lean risotto dish.

Ingredients

- 120 grams (4 oz) of dried wild mushrooms
- 300 grams (10 oz) of Arborio rice
- 3 cloves of garlic
- 450 ml (15 oz) of chicken stock
- A dash of tomato puree
- A small bunch of parsley
- A bunch of chives
- 1 tablespoon (20 ml) of extra virgin olive oil
- Salt and pepper

Serves 4

Preparation

Remove any bones from the leftover chicken.

Peel and crush the garlic.

Chop the chives finely.

Put the olive oil into the pressure cooker and heat on medium fire.

Add the Arborio rice and the crushed garlic and keep cooking while stirring continuously for 2 minutes.

Add the leftover chicken and the chives and cook for another 2 minutes stirring continuously.

Add the stock and a dash of tomato puree.

Season and stir, then seal the pressure cooker and cook for 15 minutes.

In the meantime, chop the parsley.

Let the pressure cooker cool, add the parsley and cook for another 3 to 5 minutes, until the stock has been fully absorbed by the rice before serving.

Recipe 44 – Mutton and Mushroom Stew

Mutton is another cut of meat which can be very lean, especially of it has had the chance to lead a healthy and active life. Here is a great way of cooking it with your pressure cooker.

Ingredients

- 400 grams (13 oz) of mutton, cut into bite size pieces
- 300 grams (10 oz) of potatoes
- 60 grams (2 oz) of dried wild mushrooms
- 150 ml (1/4 pint) of beef stock
- 150 ml (1/4 pint) of chicken stock
- A large onion
- A medium carrot
- A stalk of celery
- 15 bay leaves

- 5 cloves of garlic
- A glass of red wine
- A tablespoon (20 ml) of extra virgin olive oil
- A few leaves of fresh sage
- A teaspoon (5 grams) of dried thyme
- A teaspoon (5 grams) of dried rosemary
- Salt and pepper

Serves 4

Preparation

Soak the wild mushrooms in warm water for 15 minutes.

Peel and chop the onion finely.

Peel and crush the garlic.

Cut the celery into very small bits.

Peel and cut the carrot into very small bits.

Put the oil in your pressure cooker and heat on medium fire.

Add the bay leaves, the onion, the garlic, the celery and the carrot to the oil, stir and sauté for 10 minutes.

Add the game mutton meat and cook for another 5 minutes.

Add the glass of wine and cook for 3 more minutes.

In the meantime, drain the wild mushrooms.

Add the potatoes and the mushrooms.

Add the stock, the sage leaves and the thyme, the rosemary, season and stir.

Cook for 30 minutes before serving.

Recipe 45 – Steamed Red Cabbage

Here is a great side dish, full of antioxidants and very low in calories.

Ingredients

- A medium sized red cabbage (about 400 grams or 13 oz)
- 3 large red onions
- A tablespoon of extra virgin olive oil
- A cup (200 ml) of water
- Salt and pepper

Serves 4

Preparation

Slice the cabbage into thin strips.

Chop the onion very thinly.

Put the olive oil in your pressure cooker and heat it on medium fire.

Add the onion and sauté for 10 minutes.

Add the cabbage.

Add the water.

Season and stir.

Put the lid on your pressure cooker and cook for 15 minutes before serving.

Recipe 46 – Lentil and Chicken Soup

We have already seen how lentils are very good for your diet; this is an original recipe to give you lots of flavor, proteins and little fat.

Ingredients

- 300 grams (10 oz) of dry green lentils
- 100 grams (3 oz) of lean chicken meat
- 300 grams (10 oz) of potatoes
- 1 large onion
- 4 cloves of garlic
- 300 ml (1/2 pint) of chicken stock
- 300 ml (1/2 pint) of vegetable stock
- A bunch of dill
- 1 tablespoon (20 ml) of extra virgin olive oil
- Salt and pepper

Serves 4

Preparation

Soak the lentils in water for about 1 hour.

Peel and chop the onion finely.

Peel and crush the garlic.

Cut the chicken meat into very small cubes.

Put the olive oil into the pressure cooker and heat on medium fire.

Add the onion and garlic and sauté for 10 minutes.

In the meantime, drain the lentils and peel and cut the potatoes into cubes (1 inch or about 2.5 cm in size).

Add the stock and season.

Add the lentils, the chicken and cubed potatoes.

Stir and seal the pressure cooker.

Cook for 20 minutes.

In the meantime, chop the parsley.

Let the pressure cooker cool, remove the lid, add the dill and cook for another minute before serving.

Recipe 47 – Quorn Chicken and Spinach

If you have not tried *Quorn* chicken, you don't know what you are missing; apart from being much healthier and leaner than real chicken, it is much juicier too! Try it in this simple recipe.

Ingredients

- 250 grams (8 oz) of *Quorn* chicken pieces
- 300 grams (10 oz) of baby spinach leaves
- 200 grams (7 oz) of potatoes
- 120 grams (4 oz) of garden peas
- A cup (200 ml) of semi skimmed milk
- A tablespoon (20 grams) of plain flour
- A cup (200 ml) of vegetable stock
- A large onion
- A tablespoon (20 ml) of extra virgin olive oil
- Salt and pepper

Serves 4

Preparation

Peel and chop the onion thinly.

Put the oil in your pressure cooker and heat on medium fire.

Add the onion and sauté for 10 minutes.

In the meantime, peel and cut the potatoes into cubes (2 cm or 1 inch in size).

Add the potatoes and the flour and stir well.

Add the milk and the stock.

Season and seal the pressure cooker.

Cook for 15 minutes.

Let the pressure cooker cool and remove the lid.

Add the *Quorn* chicken, the peas and the baby spinach leaves.

Stir and put the lid back on.

Cook for another 10 minutes before serving.

Recipe 48 – Bean Casserole

This vegetarian casserole, made with many different types of beans, is really filling and it has very, very few calories.

Ingredients

- 150 grams (5 oz) of red kidney beans
- 150 grams (5 oz) of cannellini beans
- 150 grams (5 oz) of butter beans
- 150 grams (5 oz) of black beans
- 150 grams (5 oz) of mung beans
- 300 grams (10 oz) of chopped tomatoes
- A large onion
- A celery stalk
- 2 cloves of garlic
- A chili pepper

- 300 ml (1/2 pint) of vegetable stock

- A tablespoon (20 ml) of extra virgin olive oil

- Salt and pepper

Serves 4

Preparation

Peel and chop the onion finely.

Peel and crush the garlic.

Cut the celery into very small pieces.

Cut the chilli pepper in the middle, remove the seeds and chop it finely.

Heat the extra virgin olive oil in your pressure cooker.

When the oil is sizzling, add the onion, the celery, the garlic and the chilli.

Sauté for 10 minutes.

Add all the beans, the chopped tomato, the stock and season.

Stir and seal the pressure cooker.

Cook for 20 minutes before serving.

Recipe 49 – Chicken in Light Pepper Sauce

Here is a wonderful way of giving chicken flavor without adding calories.

Ingredients

- 400 grams (13 oz) of chicken breasts
- 3 red peppers
- A large onion
- 5 cloves of garlic
- A bunch of parsley
- A cup (200 ml) of semi skimmed milk
- A cup (200 ml) of vegetable stock
- A tablespoon (20 ml) of extra virgin olive oil
- A teaspoon (5 mg) of paprika powder
- A tablespoon (20 grams) of plain flour
- Salt and pepper

Serves 4

Preparation

Cut the chicken breasts into bite size chunks.

Peel and chop the onion finely.

Cut the peppers in two, remove the seeds and slice them.

Peel and crush the garlic.

Heat the oil in your pressure cooker, add the peppers, the onion and the garlic and sauté for 10 minutes.

Add the flour and mix well.

Add the milk and the vegetable stock.

Seal the pressure cooker and cook for 15 minutes.

Remove the lid once you have let the pressure cooker cool down.

Add the chicken breasts and the paprika.

Season and mix well.

Seal the pressure cooker and cook for 10 more minutes before serving.

Garnish with freshly chopped parsley.

Recipe 50 – Spicy Pollock Fillets

Ingredients

- 4 Pollock fillets, boned and scaled
- A large onion
- A carrot
- 5 cloves of garlic
- 6 bay leaves
- A medium ginger bulb
- 3 small shallots
- 2 lemongrass sticks
- 2 chili peppers
- A bunch of thyme
- 600 ml (1 pint) of vegetable stock
- A lemon
- A bowl of mustard

- A bowl of tartar sauce
- Salt and pepper

Serves 4

Preparation

Peel the onion, the garlic and the carrot.

Peel and cut the shallots into rounds.

Chop the thyme finely.

Peel and slice the ginger bulb.

Put the sea Pollock fillets at the bottom of your pressure cooker.

Add the stock and season.

Add the onion, the shallots, the carrot, the garlic, the bay leaves to the stock.

Add the chopped thyme.

Add the chilli peppers (as they are, do not cut them).

Add the lemongrass sticks and the ginger.

Seal the pressure cooker and cook for 15 minutes.

Allow the pressure cooker to cool and remove the lid.

Remove the Pollock fillets and drain the, before serving them with a bowl of mustard, a lemon and a bowl of tartar sauce.

Recipe 51 – Risotto and Prawns

Here is a wonderful seafood risotto with very low calorie content.

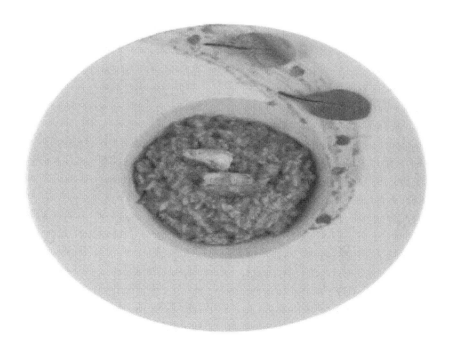

Ingredients

- 18 grams (6 oz) of dried wild prawns
- 300 grams (10 oz) of Arborio rice
- 3 cloves of garlic
- 450 ml (15 oz) of chicken stock
- A dash of tomato puree
- A chili pepper
- A glass of white wine
- A small bunch of parsley
- 1 tablespoon (20 ml) of extra virgin olive oil
- Salt and pepper

Serves 4

Preparation

Rinse the prawns in cold water.

Peel and crush the garlic.

Cut the chilli pepper in the middle and remove the seeds.

Chop the chilli thinly.

Put the olive oil into the pressure cooker and heat on medium fire.

Add the Arborio rice and the crushed garlic and chilli and keep cooking while stirring continuously for 2 minutes.

Add the prawns and cook for another 2 minutes stirring continuously.

Add the stock and a dash of tomato puree.

Season and stir, then seal the pressure cooker and cook for 15 minutes.

In the meantime, chop the parsley.

Let the pressure cooker cool, add the parsley and cook for another 3 to 5 minutes, until the stock has been fully absorbed by the rice before serving.

Recipe 52 – Barley Soup with Capelli D'Angelo

Here is a very light soup which will help you lose weight fast.

Ingredients

- 300 grams (10 oz) of dry barley
- 100 grams (3 oz) of *capelli d'angelo* (a thin type of pastina)
- 300 grams (10 oz) of potatoes
- A medium carrot
- 1 large onion
- 3 cloves of garlic
- 300 ml (1/2 pint) of chicken stock
- 300 ml (1/2 pint) of vegetable stock
- A bunch of spring onions
- 1 tablespoon (20 ml) of extra virgin olive oil
- Salt and pepper

Serves 4

Preparation

Soak the barley in water for about 1 and a half hour.

Peel and chop the onion finely.

Peel and crush the garlic.

Peel and cut the carrot into thin roundels.

Put the olive oil into the pressure cooker and heat on medium fire.

Add the onion, the carrot and garlic and sauté for 10 minutes.

In the meantime, drain the barley and peel and cut the potatoes into cubes (1 inch or about 2.5 cm in size).

Add the stock and season.

Add the barley and cubed potatoes.

Stir and seal the pressure cooker.

Cook for 20 minutes.

In the meantime, chop the spring onions.

Let the pressure cooker cool, remove the lid, add the spring onions and *capelli d'angelo* and cook for another 5 minutes before serving.

Recipe 53 – Lancette in Chicken Stock

This is an extra light dish which is ideal on cold evenings when you do not fancy a large meal; alternatively, it can be served as a starter.

Ingredients

- 200 grams of *lancette* (a type of pastina)
- 600 ml of chicken stock
- A large onion
- A medium carrot
- 3 bay leaves
- A large potato
- A teaspoon (5 grams) of dried parsley
- A stalk of celery
- 2 garlic cloves
- Salt and pepper

Serves 4

Preparation

Peel the onion, the carrot and the garlic.

Peel and cut the potato into 4 big pieces.

Put the stock in your pressure cooker.

Put the onion, the garlic, the carrot and the potato into the stock.

Add the bay leaves and season.

Seal your pressure cooker and cook for 10 minutes.

Allow the pressure cooker to cool and add the *lancette*.

Seal the pressure cooker again and cook for another 10 minutes.

Remove the lid (after having allowed the pressure cooker to cool down) and add the dry parsley.

Cook for 2 more minutes before serving.

Recipe 54 – Spicy Beef Tomatoes

Here is a simple recipe with very few calories yet packed with antioxidants; tomatoes can be used as a side, but as they are quite 'meaty', they can easily replace meat on your dinner table.

Ingredients

- 4 large beef tomatoes
- 2 chili peppers
- About 20 basil leaves
- 12 anchovies
- 12 pitted olives
- A tablespoon (20 grams) of dry oregano
- A tablespoon (20 ml) of extra virgin olive oil
- Salt and pepper

Serves 4

Preparation

Wash and cut the beef tomatoes horizontally.

Salt the cut side and place them face down on a plate for about 15 minutes; the tomatoes will lose some juice; keep it.

Insert 3 olives and 3 anchovies into each tomato.

Heat the oil in your pressure cooker on low fire.

In the meantime, chop the basil leaves finely.

Season the tomatoes with the chopped basil and with the dry oregano.

Add some pepper and a bit of salt if necessary.

Place the tomatoes in your pressure cooker, face up.

Add the juice of the tomatoes, seal the pressure cooker and cook for 7 minutes.

Let the pressure cooker cool, remove the lid and turn the tomatoes cut face down.

Reseal the pressure cooker and cook for 5 more minutes before serving.

Recipe 55 – Corn Chowder

We have already seen how corn is very good to lose weight, as it has almost no calories; of course, if you want to make it tasty, you will need to add some other ingredients; this corn chowder does just that!

Ingredients

- 200 grams (7 oz) of corn
- A large onion
- A stalk of celery
- 120 grams of potatoes
- 5 spring onions
- A teaspoon (5 grams) of dried thyme
- 600 ml (1 pint) of semi skimmed milk
- 300 ml (1/2 pint) of vegetable stock
- A bunch of parsley
- A tablespoon (20 ml) of extra virgin olive oil
- Salt and pepper

Serves 4

Preparation
Peel and chop the onion finely.

Cut the celery into small bits.

Peel and cut the potatoes into small cubes (1 cm or ½ in h in size).

Wash and cut the spring onions.

Put the olive oil in your pressure cooker and heat on medium fire.

Add the chopped onion and sauté for 10 minutes.

Add the corn, the potatoes, the celery, the spring onions, the stock and the milk.

Season and stir.

Cook for 20 minutes.

In the meantime, chop the chives coarsely.

Allow the pressure cooker to cool, add the chives and cook for 3 more minutes before serving.

Can I Ask a Favour?

If you enjoyed this book, found it useful or otherwise then I'd really appreciate it if you would post a short review on Amazon. I do read all the reviews personally so that I can continually write what people are wanting.

Thanks for your support!

Printed in Great Britain
by Amazon